Animals in the Forest

Written and illustrated by **Jasmine Chapgar**

through **Sheppard Software**

www.sheppardsoftware.com

Copyright © 2020 Jasmine Chapgar

Summary: A book to teach kids about the forest and the animals that live there
ISBN: 9781090636683

Educators, librarians and parents, for a variety of teaching tools
please visit our free educational website: https://www.sheppardsoftware.com
and videos here: https://www.youtube.com/user/SheppardSoftwareCom

Text, design and illustration by Jasmine Chapgar at Sheppard Software,
adapted from the online movie "Animals in the Forest".

To all the kids out there –

Always remember:
spend lots of time outdoors in nature
be kind to all people, animals, plants & bugs
protect the planet & the environment
reduce, reuse & recycle
keep a love of animals & nature as you grow up!

Have you ever been to a forest?

Forests are usually full of plants and grass...

Forests are also the home of lots and lots of animals!

What kinds of animals can you find in a forest?

Chipmunks are some of the smallest animals in the forest. They can be even smaller than flowers!

You may see these furry animals on the ground, looking for food or eating.

Sometimes you might also see chipmunks in a tree if they are trying to hide from something.

A raccoon is another furry animal that lives in the forest.

They look like they are wearing black masks on their eyes

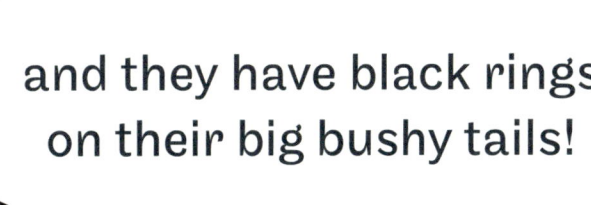

and they have black rings on their big bushy tails!

Raccoon paws are similar to your hands. They use their paws to hold things, and climb trees.

Have you heard birds singing? If you listen, you can hear them whistling to each other!

Owls are a special kind of bird that live in the forest. They usually sleep during the day ...

...and wake up at night! They have big round eyes that help them see in the dark. They fly very quietly.

You may hear their hooting noises at night!

Fish are animals that live in water. If a forest has a stream or river, you may see fish swimming there.

Fish are special because they can breathe underwater!

Around a stream, you may see frogs.
Frogs are animals that usually live near water.

Frogs move by swimming
and jumping around.

You may have seen rabbits hopping around in your own backyard!

They have long ears that are very good for listening!

Skunks have long black and white fur and huge fluffy tails.

When they are scared, they spray a smell to defend themselves.

And there you have it! These are some of the animals you might find in the forest. Which one is your favorite?

Find related games, movies and activities at our free, educational website :

www.sheppardsoftware.com

 Hundreds of educational games and activities for kids and everyone to play online - and free! 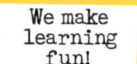 We make learning fun!

 usa  world  animals  vocab  health  science 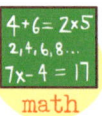 math  preschool  kids corner

In addition to our vast animal section, we have many more games and activities for topics such as:

Colors • Early Math • Shapes • Paint/Create

Preschool/Kindergarten • ABCs

Science • Geography • Math • Brain games

Health • Language Arts • Grammar

& much more!

Ages range from preschool to adult.

Also visit youtube for our educational videos on the go!

 www.youtube.com/user/SheppardSoftwareCom

Made in United States
Troutdale, OR
11/30/2024

25555586R00017